THE MAGIC WITHIN

BELONGS TO

DEAREST CHILDREN,
WAIT FOR IT

TO MY LITTLE
BROWN CHILD

A TALE OF AFFIRMATIONS & BELONGING

DR. RDM

MY FEARLESS BROWN CHILD, BEFORE THAT,
WE MUST RAISE YOU TO THE SKY

"I BELONG HERE"
YOU WHISPER

"I BELONG HERE"
YOU COMMAND

"I BELONG HERE"
YOU SHOUT

I BELONG HERE

मेरा वास्ता यहां से है

Tôi thuộc về đây

HALKAAN AYAAN KA TIRSANAHAY

నేను ఇక్కడికి చెందినవాడిని

MA PLACE EST ICI

我属于这里

আমি এখানকার

PERTENEZCO AQUÍ

હું અહીંનો છું

אני שייך לכאן

ABU M EBE A

நான் இங்கே சேர்ந்தவன்

ਮੈਂ ਇੱਥੇ ਦਾ ਹਾਂ

NO'U MAANEI

NABIBILANG AKO DITO

ฉันอยู่ที่นี่

أنتمي هنا

میں یہاں کا تعلق رکھتا ہوں۔

ഞാൻ ഇവിടെയാണ്

www.ingramcontent.com/pod-product-compliance
Lightning Source LLC
Chambersburg PA
CBRC100101100526
44582CB00014B/187